HEALTHY
FIRST FOODS FOR
YOUR BABY

The essential recipe book of solid foods for 4-12 months

Caitilin Finch

Grub Street • London

641.56222

Published in 2006 by
Grub Street
4 Rainham Close
London
SW11 6SS
Email: food@grubstreet.co.uk
Web: www.grubstreet.co.uk

A CIP block for this book is available from the British Library

ISBN 1 904943 68 3

Printed and bound in Spain

Disclaimer
The information contained in these pages has been written only from my experiences as a mother, not as a nutritionist and is not intended to replace any professional medical advice and should not be used as a basis for diagnosis or choice of treatment. Reactions to different foods will be different for everyone and answers to specific food allergies may not apply to everyone. If you're worried, see your GP immediately.

Dedication
To our beautiful children, Skylar and Mia, with love....

Acknowledgements

I have great pleasure in thanking the following people for the creation of my book.

I would firstly like to thank my wonderful husband Rob and two amazing daughters. So thank you Rob for your constant support, encouragement and giving me the motivation I needed to get my book finished, without which I can say I would probably still be only half way through completion! My children Skylar and Mia were my real inspirations and guinea pigs, without them I would never have written this book. It was through having them and bringing up my own family that my eyes were opened to this whole new world, also thanks for eating my food and testing it all for me! I would like to thank our friends and families for all their support and encouragement throughout my project. In particular I am truly thankful to my mum who taught me not only how to cook but to enjoy and take great pleasure in cooking and therefore instilling my passion for food with all her delicious meals. Not only to her but to both my mum and papa for my healthy, fun and natural upbringing which helped shape the way I rear my own family and my attitudes towards healthy eating.

I would like to say a huge thanks to Sophia for her time and perfect photographs which helped bring my book together in just the way I imagined and hoped it would look. Also a big thank you to Rod Buckle from Habana Productions for taking the time to talk to me, look at my work and offer invaluable advice and encouragement. I would like to thank my local health visitor for her help and advice.

Also to Anne Dolamore and Grub Street Publishers for believing in me and therefore publishing my book.

Finally a big thank you to Tommee Tippee for their fantastic tableware and in particular their PR manager Avril Deane for all her assistance, positive encouragement, support and advice throughout the whole project.

Contents

Introduction

Mealtimes are a fun and enjoyable experience, not just for your baby, but for both of you. This event will grow to be something you share together. It is however, not only a bonding experience but if you allow your child to be creative with their food, they will grow up to be less fussy eaters. This may turn into a mess, but as long as you realise it can all be wiped away, it does not need to become stressful. You may not think that squashing porridge between your fingers or smearing banana on the plate is fun but your baby is now experimenting with the feel, taste and smell of everything. Mealtimes are no exception, they are just one of the new experiences your child will love.

At about 4–6 months, your baby's body begins to require more iron and other nutrients than milk alone provides and it is therefore a good time to start to feed your baby cereals. Rice cream is very useful and is therefore included in many of my recipes. It is not only easily digested but gives pureed fruits and vegetables a nice consistency for delicate mouths.

I am the eldest of four siblings. We were brought up on a varied, nutritious and healthy vegetarian diet, and from a very young age I loved helping my parents, not only with the cooking, but also the growing and harvesting of the fruit, vegetables, milk, eggs, honey and grains. Now as a mother of two, my husband and I both decided to bring up our own children on a vegetarian diet. It is for this reason I have not included any recipes containing meat or fish in my book. If you do eat meat and fish I would not recommend adding it to their meals until they are at least 9–12 months old, as their systems are still too delicate to digest it. **ALWAYS** make sure that the chosen meat or fish is thoroughly cooked before giving it to your child, and at all times read the cooking instructions on the packaging carefully.

I have always enjoyed cooking and this didn't change after having my two children. More and more often I found friends and family asking me what I thought they should feed their weaning babies. Many of the recipes in my book I learnt from my mother, others I came across and developed myself whilst experimenting with different foods when my first child, (now four years of age) was a baby, and then others when my second child (now two years old) was at weaning age. They are all yummy.

healthy and nutritious first foods to give your child. As your family grows up the recipes can be adapted to suit changing tastes and needs, therefore ensuring the best diet for everyone, regardless of their age.

I often find parents telling me that they do not have enough time to cook fresh meals for their baby, especially if they have older children as well. However, you will see that the following recipes are simple to make and there will be more than enough for one meal. Instead of wasting the left-overs or freezing it all, a very useful method I have found is to put the surplus into ice cube trays and then freeze. This way you will have a variety of ready-made meals to hand which you can then simply defrost the number of cubes required, either on the hob with some extra water or in a microwave. If extra water is added, the meal may become runny, so I recommend adding a small amount of baby rice after defrosting.

If a recipe is suitable for freezing there is an * next to the recipe title at the top of the page.

With a little knowledge and awareness a nutritious diet is easy to prepare. Achieving this balanced diet for your little one does not have to be difficult or expensive. Starting your baby on a healthy diet is in many ways very beneficial. It is at these early stages in life that your child is rapidly growing and vital parts of their body and brain are forming. We can help this by feeding them nutritious, balanced meals. If we set a precedence early on, there is much less likelihood of problems arising later on. Also by introducing different tastes, textures and colours from an early age in the weaning process it can help to ensure less fussy eaters later – I however cannot promise this will be the case, but it will definitely help!

We all know how frustrating it can be when you have a cupboard full of raw ingredients, but cannot find inspiration as to what to make, so I decided to overcome this by creating tables you can use when you have certain ingredients in the cupboard and are unsure of what to make with them. Use the tables on pages 60-62 to read off the ingredients and see which recipes are suitable and vice versa.

With an abundant supply of fresh fruit, vegetables, nuts, grains, pasta and herbs now available to us throughout the year, there are numerous possibilities for imaginative and enticing meals. These recipes will therefore appeal to all children alike.

I hope you enjoy making the following recipes for your babies as much as I did. I am confident that they will delight in them just as much. Happy cooking.

A Basic Healthy Food Cupboard and Quick Nutritional Guide

The following few pages give some ideas of the essentials for a nutritious, well-stocked food cupboard. The following foods will play a crucial part in any healthy baby, child or adult's diet. I would always recommend using organic fruit and vegetables, but it is not necessary or essential. If you use non-organic produce it needs to be thoroughly washed prior to use as there are always pesticide residues left on the surface. As well as washing your fruit and vegetables you should always wash your hands before handling or cooking meals for your little ones.

Salt

First an important note about salt.

Babies and young children need little or no salt. Tiny babies simply cannot cope with much as it poisons their kidneys. It can also make your child nervous and irritable.

A baby has very acute taste buds, what may appear bland and tasteless to an adult will of consequence be full of flavour to a baby. The fresh foods used to make the meals in this book contain enough natural salt themselves. For these reasons you do not need to add any salt to your baby's meals.

Vegetables

Vegetables should form a huge part of one's diet and as there is so much choice today meals can be made interesting, colourful and very tasty. They provide an abundance of vitamins, iron and folic acid, as well as an important base for starch and complex carbohydrates in a meal (see potatoes).

Green leafy vegetables are excellent sources of iron, folic acid and C and B group vitamins.

Even if your child dislikes most vegetables and turns their nose up at them, try carrots as they contain a huge range of vitamins and are often said to be the 'most important vegetable'. Children tend to like carrots due to their sweet flavour.

Other vegetables that are very useful as base ingredients include sweet potatoes, squash and parsnips. Children really like them due to their sweet, mild flavours and soft, easy-to-eat textures.

Tomatoes are perfect for mixing with other vegetables and pulses or to be used as a base for a sauce. When blended down they then have an appealing colour and also provide a host of good vitamins. Salad ingredients are really good raw and are therefore perfect finger foods from six months onwards.

Dairy Products

Dairy produce is available in abundance today and is in many forms. It is a very important source of protein (especially for vegetarians who include them in their diet). Children should always include milk of some kind in their diets, whether it is soy (non-dairy), cows', goats', rice milk etc. Children should not be given milk other than breast or formula as a main drink until the age of one. From this age, until the age of five children should have full fat milk in their diets because the lower fat types will fill them up without providing all the correct nutrients. It can however be used from the age of 6 months onwards in small quantities when creating your babies' meals. By the time they reach five it is okay to give them semi- or skimmed milk.

Cheese is also a very popular food with young children; it can be eaten with a number of meals or simply as a finger food.

Note: Some children are lactose intolerant which means that they cannot have milk or any foods containing milk.

Fats and Oils

Fats and oils are important in our diets; they contain high levels of vitamins such as A, D and E. Oils high in polyunsaturates such as sunflower, rape seed and ground nut oil are good for general use. Whereas oils high in monosaturates, such as olive oil, are thought to reduce cholesterol levels. I find olive oil to be a favourite due to its soft flavour and therefore tend to use it readily in my cooking.

It is important to realise that babies have small tummies and need energy to grow. It may be a good idea to cut down on fats for adults but not for children.

Fruit

Children should be encouraged to eat a lot of fruit and drink pure fruit juices, for younger babies juices should be diluted down to 1 part pure fruit juice to 10 parts water.

Now, with fresh fruits readily available all year round, the choices to give your little ones have expanded greatly. Fruits are a vital (and easy) component to all healthy diets and children of all ages love them. Bananas, for example (often a favourite, with even the smallest of babies, due to their sweetness and soft texture), not only hold vital minerals and vitamins such as potassium, they also supply plenty of energy.

There are numerous recipes based around fruits, from a crumble, down to a simple fruit salad or fruity milkshake. All of which are a tasty, healthy treat, snack, or even meal for your child. I always seem to find myself with some sort of fruit (dried or fresh) in my bag or in the car, ready to hand when my children say those words "I'm hungry" and here we have it, the perfect healthy, instant snack.

Herbs and Spices

Both fresh and dried herbs are readily available to buy. If using dried, freeze-dried is best, otherwise buy in small quantities and replace regularly. Herbs not only add flavour to an otherwise plain or boring dish, they are also high in valuable minerals and vitamins.

Spices are often thought of as hot and therefore not suitable for your baby, this however is a misconception. Spices add warmth and colour to your little meals and your baby will love the difference they make. You don't have to use them all the time but they can vary meals that may otherwise become repetitive. Cumin and turmeric are good. Turmeric not only gives a lovely flavour, and a bright yellow colour, it is beneficial to the immune system.

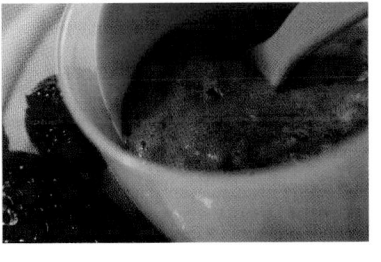

Neither do they just have to be used for savoury dishes. Sweet spices that were very popular with my children included cinnamon and nutmeg. I would simply add these to a steamed fruit puree and serve (see recipe, page 48).

Don't worry if you haven't really used a lot of spices in your cooking before, they are fun to experiment with. Add a little to begin with until you know what is right, mix various spices together and you will find combinations your baby likes.

Non-Dairy Products

Non-dairy products are essential for a vegan diet or a child with a lot of dairy allergies. They are found to be a good source of protein and the best source is in fact soy bean. Tofu (made from soy bean curd) is not only high in protein, but also in iron and B group vitamins. Even though it is a vegetable-based source of iron, it is good to include a source of vitamin C in the meal so your body can absorb the iron. Soya products often taste slightly sweeter than dairy products and if possible it is therefore nice to use both to create a variety of flavours. Due to its chewy texture your older children will like this new feeling in their mouths as they get used to eating lumpier foods.

It is recommended that your child, up until the age of four, is not given soya products more than once or twice a week.

Nuts and Seeds

Nuts must always be used with caution as in certain instances they can cause allergies, especially if there is a history of allergies in the family. Likewise oils produced from nuts may cause a reaction, so if you are unsure use an alternative such as olive oil. If you suspect your child may be allergic to something consult your doctor immediately.

It is therefore recommended that nuts and seeds should be avoided up to the age of six months. Also up until five years of age be careful with whole nuts, in case of choking.

In any case NEVER leave your child unattended whilst eating, in case of choking.

There is an abundance of different nuts and seeds available that can be bought almost anywhere. They are a very important source of calcium and protein.

Nuts and seeds are very versatile and can be crushed or finely ground and added to almost anything. In order to obtain the maximum flavour it is useful to lightly roast them first.

Pasta

Pasta is a quick and easy source of starchy, complex carbohydrate. It is easily available in numerous shapes, sizes, colours and flavours. However for my recipes you will be using the smallest of sizes which are best for little mouths. Cook your pasta in plenty of boiling water, salt is not necessary. Pasta was always and still is a favourite with my children. It is quick and easy to prepare a healthy sauce to stir in.

Perhaps sprinkled with a small amount of Cheddar cheese.

Rice

Rice is the staple food of half the world's population. It is a varied, quick and easy food to cook containing numerous valuable vitamins, minerals and proteins. It also hosts starches and complex carbohydrates. As one of the most easily digested foods, it is a very good first food for your baby. It can be used whole as your baby begins to enjoy and experiment with lumpy and textured food, but before this, rice flour is a vital ingredient. This can either be made, or bought, ready prepared as 'baby rice'.

Potatoes

Like rice and pasta, potatoes are a starchy food that should form at least half of the calorie intake of a good diet. In the case of baby foods they are extremely useful in that they are soft and easy to mix with a variety of other vegetables. They also have a mild flavour, not too intense for babies' sensitive taste buds. For natural sweetness, deep-orange sweet potatoes are a very useful ingredient and they contain more nutrients than ordinary ones.

Flours

Flours are a good source of protein and complex carbohydrates. They are available in numerous varieties for example; plain, wholemeal, buckwheat, rice etc. So when using them try to vary the types as it makes foods more interesting by providing different flavours as well as textures.

Beans and Pulses

There is a huge variety of pulses, forming over half the world's protein. Beans and pulses are cheap, very tasty and so easy to store. They are extremely nutritious, low in fats and high in dietary fibre and proteins. However, they lack one of the essential amino acids, but this one is found in grains, and therefore when eaten together they form a complete protein. So when a meal contains pulses try also to include starches so the protein circle is complete. For example; beans with rice or lentils with couscous.

Most pulses need soaking, preferably overnight and then cooking in the soaking water. They should be boiled quickly for the first 10 minutes and then simmered; this will destroy any potential toxins. They should also be cooked until completely soft to ease digestion.

The following recipes should get your babies used to a number of different flavours and colours as their food journey begins.

First Tastes 4-6 months

Babies are born with a natural supply of iron but it is at this stage that your baby's natural supply has declined and they will need it from sources other than milk.

Your baby cannot properly digest any foods other than breast or formula milk before the age of 4 months, so it is important not to introduce solid foods before at least that age. There are certain foods that cannot yet easily be digested by your baby's delicate system. In certain instances they can cause allergies, especially if there is a history of allergy in the family. Foods that are known to be best avoided up until the age of 6 months include: cow's milk, eggs, gluten (this is in wheat, barley and rye), nuts, citrus fruits.

Begin by introducing the smallest amounts of very finely pureed food a little at a time. Pureed fruit or baby rice mixed with your baby's usual milk is a good starter. Remember that this is an entirely new experience for your little ones, they are used to milk, and this first food not only has a different texture, but a spoon has also been introduced. They may spit it out straight away but don't fret as they will get used to it!

Remember that the nutritional value of the food is not that important at this stage, as milk will still provide the bulk of your little one's nutritional needs. It will continue to be the most important food source for your baby up until the age of 6 months, so one solid meal a day is adequate. Gradually introduce different tastes and enjoy this new experience together.

Avocado and Yoghurt

The smooth creamy texture of avocados perfectly combines with the yoghurt, making this a very quick, easy and healthy meal high in vitamin E.

Ingredients

1/2 ripe avocado, mashed
3 tbsp full fat plain yoghurt

1. Peel and remove the stone from the avocado, mash with a fork, or for a very smooth texture mix it in a blender for a minute.

2. Add the mashed avocado to the yoghurt, combine and serve.

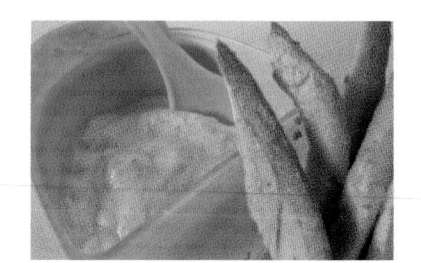

Buckwheat Porridge

Buckwheat produces a sweet and speckled gluten-free flour perfect for making this smooth, sweet and creamy porridge.

Ingredients

300ml baby's usual milk
2 tbsp fine buckwheat flour

The quantities are dependent on your child's appetite as well as the thickness you would like the porridge to be.

A sweetener is not required as the milk provides a sweetness of its own.

1. Heat the milk in a small saucepan, until warm (not boiling).

2. Add the fine buckwheat flour and cook on a moderate heat for 5-10 minutes.

3. Allow to cool before serving. At this point you can also add further milk if so required.

Cheesy Leek and Potato *

Almost like a creamy soup. I found this warm, delicious meal a favourite with my children.

Ingredients

2 tbsp olive oil
1/2 small onion, diced
1 small leek, chopped
1 medium potato, peeled and diced
4 tbsp baby's usual milk
15g Cheddar cheese, grated

1. Gently fry the onion and leek, in the olive oil for approximately 5 minutes. While this is cooking boil the diced potato in a small saucepan until soft and then drain, leaving a small amount of water. Add to the leek and onion.

2. Puree or mash with the milk.

3. Stir in the grated Cheddar cheese, allow it to melt, cool and serve.

Cheesy Spinach *

Spinach is packed with iron, essential in a healthy diet. People often assume it will be too strong for a baby, but when combined with creamy potato, a much milder flavour is created.

Ingredients

1 medium potato, peeled and diced
30g spinach

5g Cheddar cheese, grated
Baby rice (optional)

1. Peel and dice the potato. Put in a small saucepan, cover with water and boil for 15 minutes or until soft.

2. Meanwhile put the spinach in a little water (150ml), cover and simmer for 10 minutes.

3. Drain the potato and add to the spinach (keeping the water from the cooked spinach, as this retains many of the vitamins).

4. Puree this and add the grated cheese, which will melt in the warm puree.

If you find the taste is too strong for your baby it is a good idea to add the baby rice, which will tone down the flavour.

Caitilin's Tip: It's bright green so kids will love it!

Cheesy Vegetables *

Vegetables are packed with the vitamins and minerals needed for a healthy growing child. I found this combination a favourite.

Ingredients

1 tsp oil
1 small onion, chopped
1 medium carrot, diced
1 medium potato, diced

3 medium broccoli florets, halved
30g peas
2 tbsp baby's usual milk
15g Cheddar cheese

1. Fry the onion in the oil for approximately 3 minutes. Remove from the heat and put aside while you cook the other vegetables.

2. Put the carrot and potato in a saucepan with enough water to cover them. Cover with a lid, bring to the boil and cook for 15 minutes and then add the broccoli. After a further 5 minutes add the peas. Continue to cook for a further 5 minutes.

3. Remove from the heat, drain the majority of the water and add the onion.

4. Puree or mash with the milk.

5. Stir the grated Cheddar cheese, allow it to melt, cool and serve.

Easy Peasy Potato *

The smooth creamy consistency is always a favourite with new delicate mouths. Easy to make, a large quantity can be prepared at one time and then frozen.

Ingredients

2 small potatoes, peeled and diced
50g garden peas
2 tbsp milk
2 tbsp baby rice

1. Peel and chop the potatoes. Boil in 600ml water for 15 minutes and then add the peas. Cook for a further 5 minutes. Ensure the potato is now cooked until soft.

2. Drain off the majority of the water and add the milk.

3. Puree or mash, add the baby rice, allow to cool and serve.

Maize Meal Broccoli *

The creamy smooth consistency of the maize meal appeals to delicate mouths. Combined with the broccoli, a healthy, tasty meal is created.

Ingredients

50g maize meal
3 large broccoli florets, chopped

1. Put the maize meal into a small saucepan and add enough water to cover. Simmer for approximately 5 minutes, or until soft. Meanwhile steam the broccoli and put to one side.

2. Combine the soft maize meal and broccoli and mash or puree to desired consistency. Allow to cool before serving.

Caitilin's Tip: Maize meal is a really good, healthy base for any simple vegetable puree. In this recipe I have used broccoli but you can steam any vegetable and add it in place of the broccoli.

Simple Mixed Vegetables *

A hearty and tasty meal packed with vitamin C, essential B vitamins and minerals.

Ingredients

1 tsp olive oil
1 small onion, peeled and diced
1 small potato, peeled and diced
1 small carrot, peeled and diced
30g peas

1. Fry the onion in the oil for 2 minutes.

2. Boil the potato and carrot for 15 minutes and then add the peas. Cook for a further 5 minutes.

3. Drain the majority of the water and add the onion.

4. Puree or mash and serve.

Squash and Carrot *

A smooth first food that will soon become a favourite. This has a lovely naturally sweet flavour and a warm orange colour and is packed with vitamins A, B and C.

Ingredients

1 carrot, peeled and diced
1/2 butternut squash, peeled and diced
Small knob butter
2 tbsp baby's usual milk
2 tbsp baby rice

1. Boil the peeled and diced carrot and squash for 15 minutes or until soft.
2. Drain the majority of the water and add the butter and milk.
3. Puree or mash and stir in the baby rice, serve.

Sweet Vegetables *

Carrots and parsnips are easily digested and form a naturally sweet and smooth puree, ideal for a first introduction to solid foods.

Ingredients

1 medium carrot
1 medium parsnip
25g sweetcorn
Knob unsalted butter

1. Peel and dice both the carrot and parsnip.

2. Put in a small saucepan with 600 ml water, bring to the boil and allow to simmer for 10-15 minutes, or until soft.

3. Add the sweetcorn at the end for 2-3 minutes. Drain, leaving a small amount of the water they were boiled in.

4. Stir in the butter, and puree or mash to desired consistency.

Winter Vegetable Surprise

A yummy, simple yet filling meal ideal for those first tastes as it is easily digested. Always a favourite with my children.

Ingredients

1 small onion
1 tbsp olive oil
1 carrot
1 potato
3 broccoli florets, roughly chopped
2 tbsp baby's usual milk
2 tbsp baby rice

1. Peel and dice the onion and fry in the olive oil for approximately 2 minutes.

2. Peel and dice the carrot and potato, boil in a small saucepan with enough water to cover, for 10 minutes and then add the broccoli. Cook for a further 10 minutes.

3. Drain the majority of the water and add the onion. Stir in the milk. Puree or mash, add the baby rice, allow to cool and serve.

Apple and Mango *

High in vitamin C, apples and mangoes combine perfectly to create a yummy sweet pudding.

Ingredients

1 ripe apple
1 ripe mango
300ml water
2 tbsp baby rice

1. Peel and core the apple, chop and put in a saucepan with the water. Bring the water to boil, turn down and allow to simmer for 12 minutes until soft. While this is cooking, peel and slice the mango and remove the large stone, put aside.

2. Remove the apple from the heat and pour off most of the water, add the apple to the mango.

3. Puree to your desired consistency and allow to cool.

4. Add the baby rice, mix and serve.

Apple and Pear *

Apples and pears are soft and sweet, easily digested and can be eaten at any time of day, making this a perfect quick and easy recipe.

Ingredients

1 ripe apple
1 ripe pear
10g raisins (optional)
300ml water
2 tbsp baby rice

1. Peel and dice the apple and pear. Put the chopped apple, pear and raisins in a small saucepan with the water, cover and bring to the boil. Turn down heat and allow to simmer for 10 - 12 minutes, until the fruits are soft.

2. Remove from the heat and drain off most of the water.

3. Puree to your desired consistency and add the baby rice, mix and allow to cool before serving.

Apple 'n Pear Porridge *

A yummy way of making your baby's breakfast just that little bit different, as well as providing vitamin C found in the fruits.

Ingredients

1 apple
1 pear
25g raisins (optional)
Pinch cinnamon (optional)
300ml water
Oats or ready-made oat cereal (quantity depends on the appetite of your child)

1. Peel and core the apple and pear.

2. Slice and put in a saucepan of water with the raisins and cinnamon (if desired).

3. Cover and bring to the boil, then gently simmer for 10-15 minutes, until the fruit is soft.

4. Drain off the majority of the water, cool and puree the softened fruit to your child's desired consistency.

5. Add to the ready-made oat cereal and stir. If using oats add them to the puree and cook over a slow heat for a further 5-10 minutes (at this point a small amount of water may be added).

Caitilin's Tip: I also found it very useful to make a large quantity of the fruit puree and freeze it in ice cube trays. At mealtimes it is easy simply to defrost the required amount with a little water and add to the oat cereal.

Banana and Strawberry

Another very quick and easy recipe that requires no cooking. My babies loved this deliciously sweet and smooth combination.

Ingredients

3-4 strawberries
1 ripe banana
2 tbsp water (optional)
2 tbsp baby rice (optional)

1. Wash and hull the strawberries. Chop them.

2. Peel the banana, chop it and put in a bowl with the chopped strawberries, mash them together, or for a very smooth mixture put them in a blender for a minute.

3. Add the water and baby rice (optional depending on how strong your child likes the flavours), mix them in and serve.

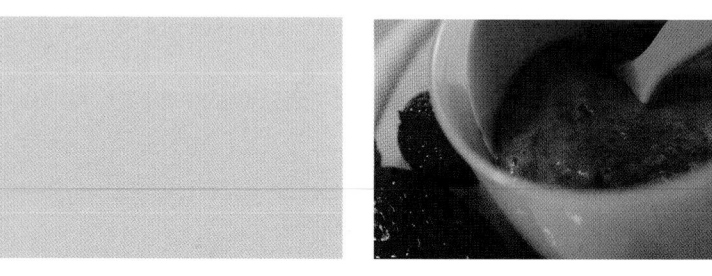

Kiwi and Banana

A very quick and easy recipe that requires no cooking, yet your baby will love the sweetness and texture of it.

Ingredients

1 ripe banana
1 ripe kiwi fruit
2 tbsp water
2 tbsp baby rice

1. Peel the banana and chop it up.

2. Peel and chop the kiwi fruit.

3. Mash them together in a bowl, or for a very smooth mixture put them in a blender for a minute.

4. Add the water and baby rice (optional depending on how strong your child likes the flavours), mix them in and serve.

Caitilin's Tip: For very young babies less than seven months, remove the small black seeds from the kiwi fruit as they can cause indigestion.

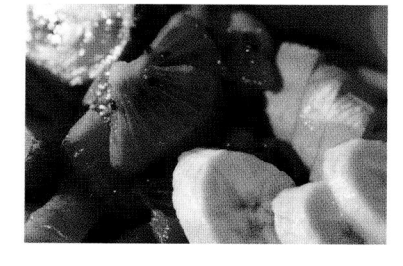

Spicy Autumn Fruits *

This versatile, yummy pudding can be eaten warm or cold. It can also be eaten as a fruity porridge, so instead of the baby rice add an instant oat cereal and serve for breakfast!

Ingredients

1 ripe apple
1 ripe pear
300ml water
Pinch cinnamon

1 ripe plum
25g raisins
2 tbsp baby rice

1. Peel and core the apple and pear, chop and put in a saucepan with the water, add the cinnamon. Bring to the boil.

2. Peel, chop and de-stone the plum and add this and the raisins to the boiling water, turn down heat and allow to simmer for 12 minutes.

3. Remove from the heat and drain off most of the water.

4. Puree to your desired consistency and add the baby rice, mix and allow to cool before serving.

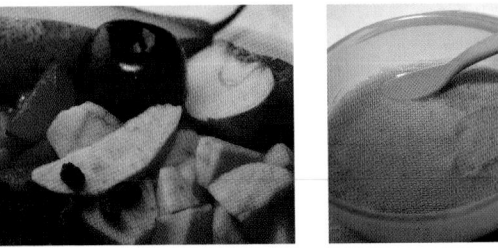

Summer Delight

A perfect, refreshing summer fruit salad. Your baby will love the naturally juicy sweet taste. It is a simple recipe that can be made quickly with no cooking required.

Ingredients

1 ripe peach or nectarine
3-4 strawberries
10 raspberries
2 tbsp water (optional)
2 tbsp baby rice (optional)

1. Peel the peach or nectarine and remove the stone, then dice the flesh.

2. Wash and hull the strawberries, chop and put in a bowl along with the diced peach and raspberries, mash them together, or for a very smooth mixture put them in a blender for a minute.

3. Add the water and baby rice (optional depending on how strong your child likes the flavours), mix them in and serve.

Lumpy Foods 6-12 months +

By now your baby may be more used to food and the whole concept of eating. It will therefore be time to start to introduce more textured meals and stronger flavours. However milk will still play a large part in your baby's diet, but iron will now be sourced from his or her solid food intake.

Foods containing gluten, eggs (thoroughly cooked), nuts and citrus fruits can be added to your baby's diet (they should be avoided until at least the age of six months). If you suspect your child has an allergy you must consult your doctor.

Between 8-12 months much more lumpy food can be given, but remember every child is different so only go at the pace of your baby. Don't give up, as it is a new experience and it will take a little getting used to, persevere but don't force.

Finger foods can be introduced during and between meals (see page 50) and by the age of 12 months your baby should by enjoying three solid meals a day, and will be joining in with the family meals.

The following recipes are suitable for 6 + months, so continue to cook and enjoy the eating experience with your new friend!

Butter Beans in Cheese Sauce *

High in protein, butter beans combine perfectly with a mild, cheesy, parsley sauce to create a meal perfect for your little one's delicate taste buds.

Ingredients

100g pre-cooked butter beans

For the cheese sauce:
300ml milk
3 level tbsp plain flour
Small knob unsalted butter
25g Cheddar cheese
1 tbsp parsley

1. Put the milk, flour and butter into a saucepan, over a medium heat. Stir continuously (this will ensure it doesn't get lumpy) for about 5 - 10 minutes, until the mixture thickens.

2. Grate the cheese and finely chop the parsley. They can now be stirred in to the sauce. The cheese will melt and slightly thicken the sauce.

3. Add the butter beans and simmer for a further 2 - 3 minutes.

4. You can now serve or blend to a desired consistency before serving.

Caitilin's Tip: If you find the sauce is too thick then add some more milk, this will thin it down.

It is nice served with grated cheese on top and some broccoli florets on the side.

Chick Pea Dinner *

A simple recipe, which provides a good source of protein for your baby. It's so yummy that you can always save the surplus and freeze it, or don't puree it and eat it yourself. This way you are introducing and encouraging your baby to eat the family meals.

Ingredients

1 small onion
1 garlic clove
1 tsp sunflower oil
250g pre-cooked chick peas
400g tin chopped tomatoes
Mixed herbs to season

1. Peel and dice the onion. Crush the garlic.
2. Slowly fry the chopped onion and garlic in the oil for approximately 3 minutes.
3. Add the remaining ingredients.
4. Allow to simmer over a medium heat, stirring well for 10-15 minutes.
5. Puree to the desired consistency, allow to cool and serve.

Couscous Risotto

The soft, delicate nature of couscous is ideal for those first really textured meals.

Ingredients

30g couscous
1/4 tsp turmeric
1/2 small onion, diced
1 tsp olive oil

2 mushrooms, finely chopped
1 carrot, grated
1/2 courgette, grated
Pinch mixed herbs

1. Put the couscous in a small pan with the turmeric, add enough boiling water to cover the couscous. Bring back to the boil. Cover, remove from the heat and set aside while you cook the vegetables.

2. Fry the onion in the olive oil, add the finely chopped mushrooms, grated carrot and courgette. Add 3-4 tbsp water and cook the vegetables until soft.

3. Add the couscous and herbs to the vegetables, stir and leave for 3-4 minutes, so that the flavours combine and the couscous continues to cook in the steam. Allow to cool and mash to desired consistency.

Caitilin's Tip: If you prefer use just carrot or courgette, or a little of each.

Dahl  *

Dahl is a really useful way to introduce your baby to spicy foods. Don't worry though it's not too hot and the spices used just give it a mild flavour.

Ingredients

100g split red lentils
1 small onion
1 garlic clove, crushed
1 tbsp olive oil
1/2 tsp turmeric
1/4 tsp cumin
1 tbsp creamed coconut, grated

20g sweetcorn
1 carrot, peeled and grated
1 tsp fresh coriander, chopped
1/4 tsp garam masala

Baby rice
1 tbsp natural full-fat yoghurt

1. Rinse the lentils and cook in 600ml water over a medium heat for 25 minutes.

2. Peel and dice the onion and fry in the olive oil with the crushed garlic for 3-4 minutes.

3. Add the turmeric, cumin and creamed coconut, stir and allow these to cook over a medium heat for a further 2 minutes.

4. Add the sweetcorn and grated carrot.

5. Add the lentils to this mixture and allow to simmer for 15 minutes (more water may be added at this point) stirring regularly. After 10 minutes add the coriander and garam masala.

6. Blend to desired consistency and stir in the baby rice.

7. Serve in a bowl with a spoonful of natural full-fat yoghurt in the middle.

Herby Mushroom Omelette

Eggs are a good source of protein and when combined with the mushrooms and herbs a yummy omelette is created.

Ingredients

1 button mushroom
10g unsalted butter
1 egg
4 tbsp baby's usual milk
Pinch mixed herbs, finely chopped

1. Peel and finely chop the mushroom.
2. Fry in the butter for 1 minute, until starting to brown.
3. Crack the egg into a small mixing bowl and add the milk and herbs.
4. Add to the cooked mushrooms. Stir continuously for 3 minutes.
5. Allow to cook for a further 1 minute and then using a spatula remove from the pan and serve.

Caitilin's Tip: Another idea would be to omit the mushroom and make a simple herby scrambled egg.

Kidney Bean Dish *

Kidney bean dish is and always has been a favourite with my two children and whole family. It is simple to make and a large quantity can be prepared at one time.

Ingredients

1 tbsp olive oil
1 small onion, peeled and chopped
1 garlic clove, crushed
1/4 red pepper, diced
1/2 small courgette, diced
240g tin red kidney beans

400g tin chopped tomatoes
2 closed cup mushrooms, diced
25g sweetcorn
1/2 tsp mixed herbs
baby rice (optional)
Cheddar cheese (optional)

1. Fry the chopped onions and crushed garlic in the oil, for 3 - 4 minutes, until soft.

2. Add the diced red pepper and courgette, and cook over a medium heat for a further 2-3 minutes.

3. Add the remaining ingredients and simmer over a low heat for a further 15 minutes, stirring regularly.

4. Remove from the heat and mash or blend to your baby's preferred consistency. Add baby rice for a thicker consistency and mellower flavour.

5. Serve with finely grated cheese (optional).

Caitilin's Tip: As a large quantity can be made you can freeze the surplus in ice cube trays or add some chilli powder to make a simple chilli which anyone can enjoy.

Pasta and Tomato Sauce

A simple, combination for a nutritious and filling meal. Children always enjoy pasta, so introduce it with a yummy healthy sauce.

Ingredients

small pasta shapes or macaroni
(quantity depends on appetite
of child)

For the sauce * you will need:
1 tbsp olive oil
1 small onion
1 garlic clove, crushed
25g sweetcorn
1/2 x 400g tin chopped tomatoes
Pinch of basil or mixed herbs to season
Cheese to garnish (optional)

1. Peel and dice the onion and fry in the olive oil in a small saucepan with the crushed garlic. Let this sweat for 2 minutes.

2. Add the sweetcorn and chopped tomatoes. Simmer for 10 minutes stirring regularly so it doesn't stick to the bottom of the saucepan. After 8 minutes add the herbs.

3. While the sauce is simmering put the pasta into another saucepan and cover with water. Cover with a lid and bring to the boil. Cook for 10 - 15 minutes, or until soft.

4. Remove the sauce from the heat and puree to a smooth paste.

5. Drain the pasta and stir into the required amount of sauce. This way the remainder of the sauce can be frozen in ice cube trays for a later date.

6. Finally garnish with Parmesan or finely grated Cheddar cheese (optional).

Tasty Lentil Stew *

A very healthy and nutritious meal, high in protein, iron and vitamin C. Introduced at 6-12 months, it will continue to form part of a healthy diet as your little one grows up. Still a favourite in my family.

Ingredients

175g dried lentils
2 button mushrooms, chopped
1 small onion, peeled and diced
1 garlic clove, crushed
1 tbsp olive oil
1 medium carrot, peeled and grated
1 stick celery, chopped

50g sweetcorn
200g tin chopped tomatoes
Pinch marjoram
Baby rice or couscous
    (amount is dependent on the
    consistency your baby likes)
Cheddar cheese, grated (optional)

1. Rinse the lentils and cover with cold water. Cover pan with a lid and bring to the boil. Boil rapidly for 10 minutes, reduce the heat and simmer for a further 35 minutes or until tender. While the lentils are cooking prepare the remaining ingredients.

2. Fry the mushrooms, onion and garlic in the oil. Add the peeled, grated carrot and chopped celery, cook for 3 minutes.

3. Add the sweetcorn, chopped tomatoes and marjoram.

4. Cover and cook on a low heat for a further 10 minutes, stirring regularly.

5. Add the lentils, stir together and simmer for a further 10 minutes. Blend to desired consistency.

6. Serve mixed with either baby rice or couscous and grated cheese on top.

Caitilin's Tip: For this recipe I have used continental lentils, but any variety will do. As your baby starts eating lumpier food substitute couscous for the baby rice.

Vegetable Lasagne *

This is a perfect recipe for all the family; it is a good way of starting to introduce the family meals to your baby's diet. It also makes it easier when cooking because you can then just make one meal for everyone.

Ingredients

3 tbsp olive oil
1 small onion, peeled
1 garlic clove
1 small courgette
40g peas
50g sweetcorn
1/2 sweet red pepper
2 small carrots
6 broccoli florets
400g tin chopped tomatoes
Mixed herbs, to season

Cheese sauce
300ml milk
9 tbsp plain flour
25g unsalted butter
20g Cheddar cheese

8 lasagne sheets
Extra grated cheese and butter
    for the top

1. Chop all the vegetables into roughly equal-sized pieces.

2. Fry the onion and garlic in the olive oil for 1 minute and add the remaining chopped vegetables (it does not matter that they all cook at different speeds

because they will eventually be baked in a moderate oven, and this ensures that they are all cooked through).

3. Add the chopped tomatoes with their juices to the vegetables, stir and finally add the mixed herbs to season. Cover with a lid and allow this to cook for 10 – 15 minutes, stirring frequently to ensure it doesn't stick.

While this is cooking make the cheese sauce.

4. Combine the milk, flour and butter in a saucepan and stir continuously (this will ensure it doesn't get lumpy) over a moderate heat until the mixture thickens. If required add more milk, this will thin down the sauce.

5. Grate the cheese; it can now be stirred into the sauce.

Now it is time to put the ingredients together in layers to make the vegetable lasagne.

6. Pre-heat the oven (200°C, gas mark 7).

7. Cover the base of a large oven-proof dish with some of the cheese sauce.

On top of that put a layer of lasagne sheets. Cover with half of the vegetable mixture, put another layer of lasagne sheets on top of this, followed by the remaining vegetables.

8. Finally lay the third layer of lasagne sheets on top and cover with the remaining cheese sauce.

9. Cover with some grated cheese and put a few small knobs of butter on top.

10. Put in the oven for 30-40 minutes. Until the top has browned and the lasagne sheets are cooked through. You can test this by inserting a clean knife and if it feels soft it is ready.

11. Cut a small portion and mash to your baby's desired consistency.

Vegetable Paella

A delicious meal packed with the goodness of seven different vegetables. Not only will it appeal to your baby, but to the entire family.

Ingredients

50g rice or baby rice
1/2 tsp turmeric
1 small onion
1 garlic clove, crushed
1 tbsp olive oil
1 carrot, peeled and grated
1/2 red pepper, chopped

2 mushrooms, peeled and chopped
1/2 x 400g tin chopped tomatoes
Pinch mixed herbs
20g peas
20g sweetcorn
Cheddar cheese (optional), grated

1. Put the rice into a saucepan, cover with water, add the turmeric and bring to the boil. Reduce the heat and simmer for 15 minutes or until soft.

2. While the rice is cooking dice the onion into small pieces and fry in the olive oil with the crushed garlic clove.

3. Prepare the carrot, red pepper and mushrooms, add to the cooking onion. Add the chopped tomatoes and 2 tbsp water. Allow to cook for 5 minutes.

4. Add the mixed herbs, peas and sweetcorn, allow this to cook over a moderate heat for a further 5 minutes, remove from the heat and puree to desired consistency.

5. Combine with the rice. Leave uncovered and simmer for a further 10 minutes, the rice will absorb the flavour and juices.

6. Allow to cool and serve with some grated cheese.

Caitilin's Tip: If your baby is not eating lumpy foods then instead of ordinary rice use baby rice.

Apple and Rhubarb Crumble *

A pudding for the whole family. Your little one will love the sweet, tangy flavour, combined with the rough textured topping.

Ingredients

1 ripe apple
300ml water
1 rhubarb stalk
Pinch cinnamon
1 tbsp honey or brown sugar
2 tbsp baby rice

Crumble topping

40g plain flour
20g butter
5g brown sugar

1. Pre-heat the oven to 180°C, gas 4. Peel and core the apple, chop and put in a saucepan with the water, bring to the boil. Chop rhubarb into 1cm pieces and add this and the cinnamon to the cooking apple. Allow to simmer for 12-15 minutes, until the fruit is soft.

While the fruit is simmering you will need to make the crumble topping.

2. Put the flour and butter in a bowl and rub together until it reaches a fine breadcrumb consistency. Add the sugar and mix together. Pour this onto a baking tray and bake in the oven for 10 minutes.

3. Remove the fruit from the heat and drain off most of the water.

4. Puree to your desired consistency and add the baby rice, mix and then add the cooked crumble mixture. Allow to cool before serving.

Caitilin's Tip: This is nice served on its own or with some homemade custard. (see recipe page 49).

Custard

Custard is a favourite pudding that can be combined with steamed, whole or pureed fruit. Babies love its smooth sweet texture and flavour.
However it is important to note that as it is made with eggs, do not give it to your baby until over the age of six months.

Ingredients

150ml milk
1 tbsp caster sugar
2 drops vanilla essence
1 egg yolk, beaten
2 tbsp cornflour

1. Combine milk, sugar and vanilla essence in a saucepan. Bring to scalding point.

2. Gradually pour onto the egg yolk, blend and return to pan.

3. Stir continuously over a gentle heat, for about 15 minutes until the custard coats the spoon and looks creamy. Remove from the heat. Put the cornflour into a small dish and add enough milk to cover it, mix it together and pour the hot custard mixture onto it. Stir and pour back into the saucepan. Cook over a moderate heat, again stirring continuously for a further 3 - 5 minutes, or until the custard coats the back of a wooden spoon. Cool before serving.

Finger Foods 6+ months

Babies may now be enjoying the new eating experience and love to hold, feel and squash their food between their fingers. It is therefore a perfect time to introduce them to finger foods. They will love the independence of being able to eat on their own.

Just ensure that you always watch them when they are eating, in case of choking and therefore never leave your child alone unsupervised with food.

The following recipes are all healthy snacks that can be eaten at any time of day, between meals when they are hungry, or during a meal. It is also good to introduce simple, peeled, chopped fruit and cooked vegetables, which require very little preparation and can be done quickly and easily.

The following recipes will make a large quantity which can be kept in sealed airtight containers ready for another day.

Apricot Fruit Bars

Apricots and dates, both high in vital nutrients and iron, combine to make a perfect naturally sweet, yet healthy snack which your supervised toddler can eat by themself.

Ingredients

60g dried apricots
40g dates
10g sunflower seeds (optional)
6 small sheets rice paper

1. Put the dried apricots, dates and sunflower seeds into a blender. Combine until the fruit is pureed and the mixture sticks together. Put to one side.

2. Place a piece of rice paper on a clean, dry surface and spoon the fruit mixture onto it.

3. Put a second piece of rice paper on top and roll the 'sandwich' to a 5mm thickness. Then using a sharp knife cut into rectangles.

Caitilin's Tip: Keep the fruit bars in a sealed container in the fridge as it keeps them firm and fresh. They can last this way for up to a month.

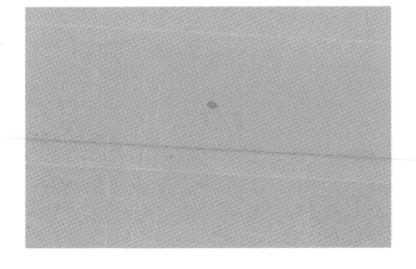
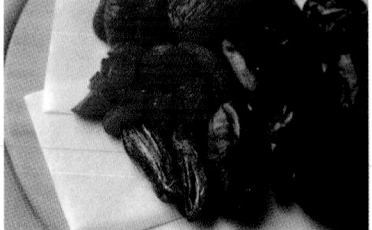

Cheesy Squares

A yummy snack, just right for in between meal times, they can be taken anywhere and are perfect for tiny hands.

Ingredients

100g plain flour
50g butter
6 tbsp cold water
20g Cheddar cheese, grated

1. Pre-heat the oven to 180°C, gas 4. Put the flour and butter into a mixing bowl and rub together until they form a breadcrumb texture.

2. Add the water and stir with a cold fork.

3. Roll out the dough on a lightly floured surface to a 10mm thickness, sprinkle on the grated cheese. Roll the cheese into the pastry, fold the pastry in half and roll out again. Fold in half a second time and roll the pastry to a 5mm thickness.

4. With either a knife or a pastry cutter cut into 3cm squares.

5. Place on a baking tray and bake in the centre of the oven for 15 minutes. Remove and allow to cool before serving.

Caitilin's Tip: It is quite useful to make these cheesy squares when you have made a pie and have some left-over pastry.

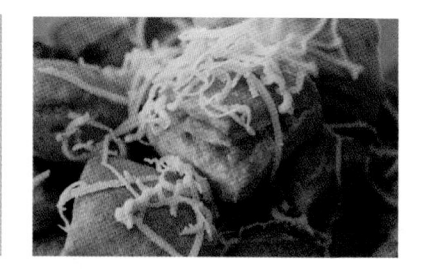

Finger Fruit Salad

The ingredients listed make enough for 3-4 children. Or you can share it with them, it's very quick, healthy and yummy.

Ingredients

1 apple
1 pear
1 banana
1 kiwi fruit
1 nectarine or peach, de-stoned, peeled and sliced

1. Simply peel and core the apple and pear. Peel all the other fruits and slice them into small wedges, arrange them in a bowl and let your child enjoy.

You can substitute any of the above mentioned fruits or add your own. Two nice summer ideas children love is to use fresh melon and strawberries. These add a cool juicy element to the salad.

Caitilin's Tip: For very young babies less than seven months, remove the small black seeds from the kiwi fruit as they can cause indigestion.

Oatcakes

This is a very handy snack to take with you when you go out, as well as having between meals at home. My mum always made them for my siblings and I, and we loved them. As we got older we would help her to cut the dough shapes out on the table, often eating the dough as we went along!

They are a brilliant healthy snack, both sugar and salt free, but energy and protein are provided by the oats and maize meal.

Ingredients

40g plain flour
30g maize meal
50g rolled oats
25g unsalted butter
100ml cold water

1. Pre-heat the oven to 200°C, gas 6.
2. Mix the flour, maize meal and oats in a mixing bowl.
3. Melt the butter in a small saucepan and mix with the water.
4. Add the water and butter mixture to the dry ingredients and stir together to form a dough.
5. Roll out the dough on a lightly floured surface (5mm thickness) and cut into shapes using a cookie cutter.
6. Place on a lightly buttered baking tray and bake in the pre-heated oven for 10 minutes. Remove and allow to cool before serving.

Caitilin's Tip: Once completely cooled the oatcakes can be stored in an air tight container for up to one week.

Rice Balls

These are an easy, healthy snack for your baby as they begin to eat textured finger foods. A good variation is to add turmeric to the rice as it is cooking and you will then have bright yellow balls!

Ingredients

30g short grain or pudding rice
Water
Pinch turmeric (optional)

1. Put the rice in a small saucepan, cover with boiling water and bring back to the boil. If you are using turmeric, add it now. Cover and simmer for 15-20 minutes, or until soft and slightly mushy.

2. Allow to cool and then slightly mash it, it will become sticky.

3. Take a teaspoon at a time and roll in the palms of your hands, to form a small ball.

4. Put on a dish in the fridge and as they cool the rice will stick together to form balls.

Snowy Fruit Balls

The perfect healthy, fun snack which can be eaten at any time of the day. It requires no cooking so is quick and easy to make.

They're yummy and everyone in my family loves them.

Ingredients

75g dried apricots
75g dried peaches
40g dried apple rings
25g sunflower seeds
50g raisins
Desiccated coconut (to roll the fruit balls in)

1. Put the dried fruit and sunflower seeds in a blender. Combine until the mixture sticks together.

2. Carefully remove the fruit mixture from the blender and using the palms of your hands, roll into small balls (2-3cm).

3. Pour the desiccated coconut into a bowl and roll each ball in it so the coconut entirely covers the surface of each one. They are now ready to eat.

Caitilin's Tip: It is best to keep the fruit balls in an air tight container in the fridge as it keeps them firm and fresh. They can last this way for up to a month.

If you do not have, or wish to omit one of the dried fruit ingredients then feel free to do so, or if you wish you can alternatively add something different. For example, some dried diced papaya, figs or dates.

Milkshakes

Homemade milkshakes are always a quick and easy nourishing drink for little ones. They are especially handy if your children don't particularly like milk, as they are a great way of making milk more fun, naturally sweeter and colourful.

Here are a number of my favourite very simple recipes:

For all of the following recipes the quantity of milk used is really dependent on the amount your baby requires, therefore the quantities I have given are only a guide.

Banana and Chocolate

1 ripe banana
200ml baby's usual milk
2 ice cubes
1 tsp cocoa powder

Put the banana, milk and ice cubes into a blender and blend until smooth. Add the cocoa powder and blend again until frothy.

Minty Chocolate

200ml baby's usual milk
1 tsp cocoa powder
3 drops mint essence

Put the milk, cocoa powder and mint essence into a blender and blend until smooth and frothy.

Strawberry

2 fresh strawberries, washed and hulled
200ml baby's usual milk

This is a really fresh and simple milkshake to make. It is completely natural and full of goodness. You simply put the strawberries and milk into a blender and blend until smooth and frothy.

Summer Fruits

2 fresh strawberries, washed and hulled
6 fresh raspberries
6 blackberries
200ml baby's usual milk
2 ice cubes

Put all the ingredients into a blender and blend until smooth and frothy.

Vanilla

1 ripe banana
200ml baby's usual milk
1 tsp vanilla essence

Put the banana, milk and vanilla essence into a blender and blend until smooth and frothy. The addition of the banana will add not only natural sweetness but also a number of vitamins and is great for energy.

4-6 Months

	Apple	Avocado	Baby Rice	Banana	Blackberries	Broccoli	Butter	Butter Nut Squash	Carrot	Cheese	Cinnamon	Coriander	Kiwi Fruit	Leek	Maize meal	Mango	Milk	Nectarine	Oats	Olive Oil	Onion	Parsnip	Pasta	Peach	Pear	Peas	Plum	Potato	Raisins	Raspberries	Spinach	Strawberries	Sweetcorn	Yoghurt
Apple and Mango	●	●														●																		
Apple and Pear	●	●																							●				●					
Apple 'n Pear Porridge	●										●								●						●				●					
Banana and Strawberry		●	●																													●		
Buckwheat Porridge																																		
Cheesy Leek and Potato										●				●			●				●							●						
Cheesy Spinach		●								●																		●			●			
Cheesy Vegetables						●				●							●			●	●					●		●						
Easy Peasy Potato		●															●									●		●						
Kiwi and Banana		●		●									●																					
Maize Meal Broccoli						●									●																			
Simple Mixed Vegetables									●												●					●		●						
Spicy Autumn Fruits	●	●									●														●		●		●					
Squash and Carrot		●					●	●	●								●																	
Summer Delight		●																●						●						●		●		
Sweet Vegetables							●	●														●											●	
Winter Vegetable Surprise		●				●			●													●						●						
Yoghurt and Avocado		●																																●

6-12 Months

Recipe	Apple	Baby Rice	Basil	Broccoli	Brown Sugar	Butter (Unsalted)	Butter Beans	Carrot	Caster Sugar	Celery	Cheese	Chopped Tomatoes	Cinnamon	Coriander	Cornflour	Chick peas	Courgette	Couscous	Creamed coconut	Cumin	Egg	Flour (plain)	Garam masala	Garlic	Honey	Kidney Beans	Lentils	Milk	Marjoram	Mixed Herbs	Mushrooms	Olive Oil	Onion	Parsley	Pasta	Peas	Red Pepper	Rhubarb	Rice	Sweetcorn	Turmeric
Butter Beans in Cheese Sauce						•	•				•											•						•						•							
Chick Pea Dinner											•					•								•						•		•	•								
Couscous Risotto								•									•	•												•	•	•	•								
Dahl	•							•						•						•	•		•	•			•					•	•							•	•
Herby Mushroom Omelette								•													•							•			•	•									
Kidney Bean Dish	•										•	•								•				•	•					•	•	•	•		•					•	
Pasta and Tomato Sauce			•								•	•												•							•	•			•					•	
Tasty Lentil Stew	•							•		•	•	•								•				•			•			•	•									•	
Vegetable Lasagne				•				•			•	•					•							•					•	•		•				•	•			•	
Vegetable Paella	•							•			•	•												•						•	•	•	•			•	•		•	•	•
Apple and Rhubarb Crumble	•	•			•	•							•									•			•													•			
Custard									•						•						•							•													

Finger Foods and Milkshakes

	Apple	Banana	Blackberries	Butter (unsalted)	Cheese	Cocoa powder	Dates	Desiccated coconut	Dried apricots	Dried apple rings	Dried peaches	Kiwi Fruit	Maize meal	Mint essence	Milk	Nectarine	Oats (rolled)	Peach	Pear	Plain flour	Raisins	Raspberries	Rice	Rice paper	Strawberries	Sunflower seeds	Turmeric	Vanilla essence
Apricot Fruit Bars							•		•															•		•		
Cheesy Squares				•	•															•								
Finger Fruit Salad	•	•										•				•		•	•									
Oatcakes				•									•				•			•								
Rice Balls																							•				•	
Snowy Fruit Balls								•	•	•	•										•					•		
Banana and Chocolate Milkshake		•				•									•													
Minty Chocolate Milkshake						•									•													•
Strawberry Milkshake															•										•			
Summer Fruits Milkshake			•												•							•			•			
Vanilla Milkshake		•													•													•

Index

Some other Grub Street books of interest

The Healthy Lunchbox
10 top lunchboxes from tots to teens
Fiona Beckett
ISBN 1904943233

Scary Dairy, Wild Wheat and Coping with Es
A Practical Approach to Children's Behavioural
Problems through Diet
Tessa Lobb
ISBN 1904943284

Kids Kitchen
100 no-knives, heat-safe recipes that children
can really make
Jennifer Low
ISBN 1904943144

Eat Smart Eat Raw
Kate Wood
ISBN 1904010121

**The Everyday Wheat-Free and Gluten-Free
Cookbook**
Michelle Berriedale-Johnson
ISBN 1898697906

The Everyday Dairy-Free Cookbook
Miller Rogers and Emily White
ISBN 190230473X

**For a complete catalogue of food and wine
books contact**
Grub Street on 020 7924 3966 or email
post@grubstreet.co.uk
www.grubstreet.co.uk